THEBOOMERLIST
1946-1964

TIMOTHY GREENFIELD-SANDERS

Luxury Custom Publishing • San Diego

CONTENTS

Introduction Jo Ann Jenkins, AARP   9

1946
Tim O'Brien   11

1947
Deepak Chopra   17

1948
Samuel L. Jackson   23

1949
Billy Joel   29

1950
Steve Wozniak   35

1951
Tommy Hilfiger   41

1952
Amy Tan   47

1953
Eve Ensler   53

1954
Julieanna Richardson — 59

1955
Maria Shriver — 65

1956
Kim Cattrall — 71

1957
Virginia Rometty — 77

1958
Ellen Ochoa — 83

1959
Ronnie Lott — 89

1960
Erin Brockovich — 95

1961
Peter Staley — 101

1962
Rosie O'Donnell — 107

1963
David LaChapelle — 113

1964
John Leguizamo — 119

PORTRAITS BY **TIMOTHY GREENFIELD-SANDERS**

INTERVIEWS BY **TOMMY WALKER, SANDRA GUZMAN, CHAD THOMPSON,** AND **TIMOTHY GREENFIELD-SANDERS**

INTRODUCTION
JO ANN JENKINS
Chief Executive Officer, AARP

The Boomer List tells the story of a generation that has uniquely influenced, shaped, and defined our world. As AARP's first boomer CEO—I was born in 1958, the same year AARP was founded—I think of the boomers as the AARP generation. Today, the oldest boomers are sixty-eight; the youngest are just turning fifty. They are an incredibly diverse generation of people who still want to live life on their own terms and make a difference and who believe they can change the world.

In this book, Timothy Greenfield-Sanders, who also gave us *The Black List*, *The Latino List,* and *The Out List*, explores the achievements, struggles, and contributions of the baby boom generation through a comprehensive look at nineteen iconic baby boomers—one born each year of the baby

boom. People like Steve Wozniak, who gave us the personal computer; Billy Joel, whose music helped define and give voice to the soundtrack of our generation; Julieanna Richardson, whose oral histories of thousands of African Americans chronicle the changed lives of the civil rights movement; and Erin Brockovich, whose environmental activism proved that one person really can make a difference.

The profiles of these nineteen boomers clearly show that they aren't done yet. They are changing and reimagining aging as they have every other stage of life they have encountered.

I think astronaut Ellen Ochoa, the first Hispanic woman in space who now serves as the Director of NASA's Johnson Space Center, said it best: "One of the things that changed during my life was I didn't feel that I was limited, that I had to make choices. You're not shut out, and you're not just cast in one particular mold."

As the boomers have transformed into the AARP generation, they refuse to be limited and to be shut out of society. They continue to break the mold—seeking possibilities over passiveness, celebrating discovery, not decline.

Timothy Greenfield-Sanders' *The Boomer List* is not just a brilliantly told chronicle of this generation. It demonstrates that boomers are still living in ways that reflect the attitudes, activism, and aspirations of their remarkable generation.

1946

JOHN WATERS

STEVEN SPIELBERG

PATTI SMITH

PRESIDENT BILL CLINTON

DIANE VON FURSTENBERG

TIM
O'BRIEN
VIETNAM VET / AUTHOR

Tim O'Brien

Vietnam was the defining event for my generation. It spilled over into all facets of American life—into music, into the pulpits, in churches of our country. It spilled over into the city streets, police forces. And even if you were born late in the generation, Vietnam was still part of your childhood. You grew up with the imagery on television. Maybe your brother served.

New York City, July 2014

By the time I had reached my senior year in college, I was adamantly opposed to the war. The best you could say about Vietnam, I thought, was that certain blood was being shed for uncertain reasons.

America was divided. My own family was divided. People were marching on the streets of Chicago, L.A., Detroit. There was stuff happening in this country that was worth rebelling against. A black guy can't sit next to you at a lunch counter? That was America.

Secretly, I thought , "Something will rescue me from this war. I won't have to be in it." I came home from a round of golf sometime around noon or so, opened the mailbox and right away saw the draft notice. I knew what it was by its color, yellow. I dropped it on the kitchen table where my mom and dad were having lunch. Probably the dominant memory on the day I die will be of that yellow piece of paper in the middle of that kitchen table and the silence that surrounded it. My mom said nothing, my dad said nothing, and I said nothing for a long time.

I worked at a meat packing plant between the time I graduated from college and went into the army. I was scared out of my mind. My dreams that summer were dreams of blood and pig stink and my future, Vietnam. I'd be talking to myself all summer long: "You could get in your car and drive to Canada and you'll be there in eight hours." And the other side of my head would say, "Yeah, but you'll look like a sissy. You'll look like a traitor. You'll be treasonous. You might end up in jail."

I just let gravity take over, got on that bus, and went into the war. I didn't have the moral stamina to say no to LBJ and Nixon and to my country. What do you call that? Well, I've called it cowardice.

The year I was in Vietnam was 1969. There were great divisions among us. We would go back to our firebase after, say, two or three weeks in the field. And the black guys would go their way and we'd go our way. However, when you got on that chopper and you headed back into the field, these were your best friends.

Two platoons, about sixty guys, myself among them, were crossing a rice patty. We were going to make a perimeter for the night. And as we're crossing the patty, one guy started singing the song "Hey Jude." And then another guy joined him. We've got these rucksacks and all the ammo we're carrying and the canteens—we made it ours. There's a line, "Don't carry the world upon your shoulders." And it felt to us as kids in our twenties that we were carrying the world on our shoulders. For just a few seconds, even in the midst of the horror, there was this beauty of this boys' choir.

I don't know if I killed anyone. Very few people ever do know. You're saying to yourself, "Dear Jesus, dear Jesus, let me live" as you're shooting your weapon. There's chaos of people running. There are mortar rounds going off all around you. Half the time your eyes are closed out of terror. But I can't cop out by saying, "Well, I don't know if I killed anybody." I was part of the war. I'm responsible. And so was all of America in the end.

> There was stuff happening in this country that was worth rebelling against. A black guy can't sit next to you at a lunch counter? That was America.

And you could say that, not just to the presidents, not just to the senators; you could say it to the Kiwanis guys so hot for the war or that housewife who was all for stopping Communism in Southeast Asia. Who wakes up every day and says, "Oh my God, we lost the war in Vietnam?" What a nightmare.

There's this mistaken notion that wars end, but they don't end. What about the women who married the veterans and had to sit through silent dinner after silent dinner? Somewhere in this country there is a ninety-five-year-old woman, probably black, who will wake up at night and say, "Where's my baby?" The answer is her baby has been dead for forty-five years. But the war is not over for that old gold-star mother. It'll never be over. And you can't expect it to be over.

You have to do something with the horror. The object in my writing is to try to salvage something from it, something in the human spirit that can prevail, that can go on. Now, all these years later, I'm an older father. I've got a nine-year-old and an eleven-year-old, and there's beauty in that world that I couldn't have imagined.

1947

GLENN
CLOSE

DAVID
BOWIE

LAURIE
ANDERSON

HENRY
CISNEROS

FARRAH
FAWCETT

DEEPAK
CHOPRA
NEW AGE GURU

Deepak Chopra

We were brought up in a Hindu family. My grandmother—if a Muslim crossed her path and the shadow of the Muslim fell on her, she would go have a shower or bath to cleanse herself. I didn't wake up to the zeitgeist until I was maybe fourteen or fifteen. There was this whole hippie crowd. We were rebels. We were totally in tune with protests against the war in Vietnam, the burning of bras in Harvard Square, and I tried my first LSD experiment.

New York City, February 2014

When I was in my final year of medical school, I got a letter saying that I could continue my training in the United States. The American doctors were all in the army, and they were in Vietnam. There was a big shortage of physicians here. At that time, there were rules in India to discourage professionals from going outside the country.

The Indian government did not allow you to leave with more than $8. But I had an uncle in London who lent me $100, so I now had $108. I decided to do something auspicious with my $108. I went to Paris, and I spent it all in one night at the Moulin Rouge. So when I got to the United States, I had no money. Zero.

I did my boards in internal medicine. I then went on to specialize in neuroendocrinology, or brain chemistry. Wherever a thought goes, a molecule follows. So your consciousness is actually governing your biology. Your emotions, your lifestyle, your personal relationships—every second they're altering your brain chemistry.

Timothy Greenfield-Sanders and Deepak Chopra (front) with members of The Boomer List *team (left to right): Graham Willoughby, Betsy Berg, Tommy Walker, Jackie Sanchez, Lauren Heanes, Sandra Guzman, Elizabeth Victorine, and Gus Sacks*

My colleagues thought I was an embarrassment because I was talking about mind, body, spirit. So I was called a quack. I was called a fraud, which I initially resented, but then I got used to it. I went to California, I gave a lecture, and they were totally different in their response to me. In fact, what I was doing resonated with the general public.

Right now, we cannot explain experience—either mental or perceptual. We don't know the two most important questions about existence: What is existence? And how come we know that we exist? There are no answers. Can we formulate a new theory of consciousness, which goes beyond the traditional way of thinking, that your consciousness is in your brain? It thinks in English with an Indian accent.

Rumi, the great poet, says, "I want to sing like the birds sing, not worrying about who hears or what they think." I question every presumption that we have about human potential. Do we have to age like everybody else is aging? I don't believe so. I think our biological age and our spiritual age are different things. And I think we can influence our biological age. (I have, by the way, all these monitors that I wear, all these sensors, that pick up biological information about me.)

What's the future? We are essentially spiritual beings having a human experience. We're citizens of the cosmos, not even of the planet with all the technologies that we have. And outer space and inner space will be great adventures.

> We're citizens of the cosmos, not even of the planet with all the technologies that we have. And outer space and inner space will be great adventures.

1948

AL GORE   DONNA KARAN   RICHARD PARSONS   STEVEN TYLER   KATHY BATES

SAMUEL L. JACKSON
ACTOR

Samuel L. Jackson

I've always been cognizant that I lived in a separate and not necessarily equal world. My whole upbringing was black. All my friends were black. All my teachers were black. Everybody I knew was black except for the people that my grandmother or my grandfather worked for. My grandparents never told me not to look white people directly in the eye. But they always said, you know, "Don't speak 'til spoken to."

New York City, June 2014

I had to watch my grandmother and my grandfather be talked to like they were less than. My grandfather was an elevator operator and he also cleaned a real estate office. They referred to him as Ed, even though some of those guys were like twenty years old and my grandfather was sixty.

My grandmother was a domestic. She worked in white people's houses like those ladies in *The Help*. And she talked about me all the time. They would give her a Christmas gift or something for me, and she would make me write a thank-you note, and I would send it back with her. So, one year, I guess when I was in about the sixth grade, something like that, I guess it took too long for me to write that thank-you note. One of the people my grandmother worked for said to her, "Pearl, did Sam get that gift?" And she was like, "Yes, sir." "I don't think we got a thank-you note from him," he said. "Y'all raising that boy right?" She took her apron off and walked out of the house, walked down the street, got on the bus and never went back.

She didn't hate white people in that way. She didn't actively tell me, "You gotta hate these white people; they're gonna do this, that, and the other thing." But when something happened she would say, you know, "That just how crackers are."

Everything that I've gone through informs me and my opinions in a way, I guess because I am a child of segregation. I lived through it. I lived in it. I was of it.

> You want to talk about me being a role model, don't talk about my characters—talk about me. I'm a good father, husband, and son.

Education was valued in my household. I started reading somewhere between three-and-a-half and four years old. So when I went to school, they understood what the expectations were in my house of me. Later, when other kids were diagramming sentences I was reading Shakespeare or *Beowulf* or whatever. When I started to read, I started to realize the world was a lot bigger place than Chattanooga, Tennessee.

The first national news that affected me happened when I was in high school. Somebody came in and whispered in the band director's ear. And he told us that President Kennedy had been assassinated. And when we got home my grandfather had all the guns out. My whole neighborhood was primed for a race war. They just knew that if Kennedy was dead, *Oh Lord*, it's about the jump off. You know, because in everybody's house there was King, Kennedy, and Jesus, the pictures on the wall, the triumvirate!

I'd walk four-and-a-half miles to school every day. From house to house we picked each other up. They weren't training us to go to Yale or Harvard or whatever. They were training us to go to Tennessee State or Fisk or maybe Morehouse.

I had applied to UCLA, UC Santa Barbara, University of Hawaii—all these exotic schools—and my mom didn't know anything about it. I was getting accepted and she finally realized what I was doing and she said, "You must be out of your mind." She pretty much grabbed me by the collar and took me to Morehouse and said, "This is where you going to school."

My cousin William, we were the same age. I went to Morehouse and William went into the army. Six months later he got shot in the head—dead. So all of a sudden, war was very real to me. I ended up meeting Stokely Carmichael and H. Rap Brown and all these guys, spending time with them and

talking to the cats who had been there about what was happening and who was really getting killed, you know, about the brothers on the front lines.

My junior year I took this public speaking course. The guy offered us extra credit if we did *The Threepenny Opera*. I didn't realize the play took place in a whorehouse. These girls are in corsets and garter belts and, *hey now!*, I've discovered my future.

With *Django Unchained*, when Quentin Tarantino told me he wanted me to play Stephen, I was like, "This is ten years too late! I'm supposed to be Django, the badass hero!" I called him back and I said, "So, in essence you want me to be the most despicable Negro in cinematic history?"

You want to talk about me being a role model, don't talk about my characters—talk about me. I'm a good father, husband, and son. I have never been arrested or gone to jail. That's not a rite of passage for every black person. I've been questioned by the police, yeah. Been run out of town by the FBI, yes. I don't advertise all the things I do. I don't take a camera crew with me to Africa to show them that I actually have dug a well. I dug a well.

I have an education. I believe in education. I read, write, I conjugate.

1949

ROBERT PALMER

VERA WANG

PAUL SHAFFER

BONNIE RAITT

LATANYA RICHARDSON

BILLY
JOEL
SINGER-SONGWRITER

Billy Joel

Our parents' generation had it a lot tougher than we did. They had to live through the Depression, World War II, and then they had to try to pick up the pieces of their lives and bring up their children. It was a great example for us. I guess we grew up with a certain amount of the ethics our parents had: Work hard, make your own way, be independent.

New York City, March 2014

I grew up in a town called Hicksville on Long Island. That's where I'm comfortable. That's who I am.

I knew when I was a little boy that I wanted to be a musician. I just wasn't sure what I would be doing specifically, whether I'd be a performer or a songwriter or a piano player or a studio guy or someone who helped produce music. And then in 1964, when I was fourteen, the Beatles came to America.

They didn't look like movie stars; they looked like working-class stiffs. They were from Liverpool, which is an even worse-sounding name than Hicksville. But my path was clear.

I hooked up with a band. We were called the Echoes. The other guys said, "You're the best singer in the band, so you be the singer." So by default, because everybody else was terrible, I became the lead singer. We played songs that I could sing—Beatles songs, Stones songs, early British invasion stuff like the Kinks and the Zombies.

The first gig we played was a church dance at the Holy Family Church in Hicksville. There was this girl there who I had a crush on. I was too shy to even talk to her—but she was looking at me. And I remember thinking, "Wow, she's looking at me! This is fantastic!"

And at the end of the night, the priest came over and gave us something like fifteen bucks each—which back then was like $1,500. I said to the priest, "You mean we get paid for this?" And that was it. That was my epiphany.

I got paid, but I never got the girl. I did write a song about her, though. Her name was Virginia. She was the girl.

When I was eighteen, I worked on an oyster boat. I'd get up at five in the morning and go out on a dredge. I was freezing. And I had these old guys making fun of me, "Oh, he's wearing gloves. Oh, the poor piano player. His hands are getting hurt." And my hands did hurt. I used to look up and see this big house on the hill, and I'd get really mad. "Bastards. They probably never worked a day in their life. They probably inherited money." Now I own that house. I am that guy. I go down to the beach and they throw me the clams. I like to help out the commercial fishermen because they can use the help.

Inspiration for writing a song comes from all over the place. The traditional way to write a song is that you take a poem and you set it to music. Well, what I do is I write the music first and then I try to figure out what was that feeling I had when I wrote that music? What is that music trying to say? Sometimes I've dreamt stuff and then, suddenly, the dream will reoccur to me. And I'll go, "Oh. That's a great idea!"

I was on a bus going down the Hudson River Line. This idea just kept coming. *I'm in a New York state of mind . . . Some folks like to get away . . .* And I'm writing this song without a piano, and I go

> Our parents' generation had it a lot tougher than we did. They had to live through the Depression, World War II, and then they had to try to pick up the pieces of their lives and bring up their children.

to this house that my wife at the time had rented, run upstairs, and the song is written in about a half hour, which I love. I love those.

Fame is a two-edged sword. You can always get a table at a restaurant, but then you really can't get through the meal without signing autographs and people taking pictures. My mom enjoys it more than me. My mom, she'll go out and she'll say, "I'm Billy Joel's mother." And I'm like, "Oh God, Mom. You're embarrassing me. Ma, don't do that." "No. It's okay. I know you don't like it, but I'm enjoying it."

I did not serve in Vietnam. I just missed being drafted, but a lot of my friends went. I don't know firsthand, but they sat me down and said, "Here's what happened." They got treated very badly, almost cast aside. There were no parades. I always wanted to welcome them home someway, which is why I came up with the song "Goodnight Saigon."

I am sixty-five this year. What am I gonna do, retire? I gotta keep my mind active or else my mind will occupy me and that's when you get in trouble. I had no idea I could continue to be a performer. I thought there was a mandatory retirement age in rock and roll. Obviously, there isn't. I'm seeing these guys—the Stones are in their seventies now. Guys like me, Springsteen—we're getting up there, in our mid-sixties. These artists just keep going and going. So, I'm just kind of doing that. That's what I do.

1950

ARIANNA HUFFINGTON

BILL MURRAY

FRAN LEBOWITZ

WILLIAM HURT

NATALIE COLE

STEVE
WOZNIAK
CO-FOUNDER, APPLE COMPUTER

Steve Wozniak

During the Fifties, the fruit orchards of Silicon Valley were going away and the homes were coming in. A lot of the kids in the neighborhood had engineers as parents. Maybe half the kids in our neighborhood were just normal kids and half of us were into electronics. I was drawing diagrams on paper and then building little devices. It turns you into kind of a nerd. Inside of me I felt like a kind of a Superman, but none of your friends know what you are, and they start socially rejecting you. Almost everyone who was deep into electronics was a social outsider.

Los Gatos, CA, April 2014

My father was strongly into ethics. And to me that meant the sum of all goodness, and the apex of all goodness was truth. I was initially for the Vietnam War, thinking we had to be for democracy. All the messages you read as a young person in high school and college were about this war. I started seeing it was really our government that was on the bad side of things and that they were the liars. So I grew up very anti-political, as did others, but I wouldn't live the full hippie life. I'd always be able to get a job, and have a home, and have a family. Those were my goals. But I admired the counter-culture thinking.

Silicon Valley started out with a few companies building transistors. The top engineers and executives would spin out of a company to start their own. That was common. Young people starting companies was unheard of back then. What Steve Jobs and I did—and Bill Gates and Paul Allen at the same time—we had no savings accounts, no friends that could loan us money. But we had ideas, and all my life I wanted to be part of a revolution. My contribution was the technology side. The companies, the rich people, they had control of the computers. We were going to take it away from them.

When Apple was going public, I gave pre-IPO stock of mine to people doing good work. Some of them had been around in the earliest days in the garage. I would not have created the great computers if I hadn't had people I was trying to impress and others pressing me, telling me, "What you are doing is great, I like what you're doing, why don't you try this?"

Finally, I had my own kids. When they were in school, I was giving the schools computers. But that's like if you have a ton of money and you give a nickel. Then I thought: What you give is the most important thing in your life, so I gave my time and wound up teaching fifth graders for eight years. I would teach them programming when they were young, not because they have to be programmers when they are older, but because you learn to think logically about life.

I'm known for a couple of things. I have to say that being recognized for inventing the personal computer and for my engineering skills are what mean the most to me.

Where is technology going in the future? I always start by looking at what I like. That's how I predict where I think the future is going to be. In the early days I was right a lot more often.

I've thought very deeply about when I die: Do I want to be a super successful person or do I want to be somebody who enjoyed my life? I've had two formulas in my life for happiness. H=S-F. Happiness equals smiles minus frowns. I also expanded it to say $H=F^3$. The first F, food, is a metaphor for the necessities of life. The second F is for fun. That's all of our entertainment. The third F is friends because if you don't have people, how are you going to be happy? Your happiness doesn't mean anything if you are just a little island.

When I was inducted into the Hall of Fame at my high school, I gave that formula. The kids all started laughing, and I realized there might be a fourth F.

> The companies, the rich people, they had control of the computers. We were going to take it away from them.

1951

ROBIN
WILLIAMS

ANJELICA
HUSTON

PATTI
D'ARBANVILLE

STING

JULIAN
SCHNABEL

TOMMY HILFIGER
FASHION DESIGNER

Tommy Hilfiger

I came from a family with nine children in a very small town with very hard-working parents who struggled to pay the bills. I never wanted to be in that position. I delivered newspapers to make money; peering in the windows I was shocked to find that certain people had swimming pools in their backyards and housekeepers. I thought, "Wow, I want to live like that."

New York City, February 2014

I couldn't play an instrument or sing, but I wanted to look like a rock star. And I knew there were a lot of other people out there who wanted the same. I told my father I wanted to open a shop and he laughed. "How far do you think this thing will go?" And I said, "Well, it's not that this thing is gonna go, but I'm gonna go." "Come on, don't be ridiculous. With that long hair, nobody would hire you anyway."

I moved to New York, and I set up a company called Tommy Hill. I went to the Gap, cut the labels out, put my label in, and changed them. I packed them in a duffel bag and I went to Bloomingdale's and to Saks Fifth Avenue and all these stores and I sold my line to them.

There are very few real designers who invent. The pant was invented a very long time ago. And we redesign it. We make it shorter, we make it longer, add pockets, take them away. I'm not embarrassed to call myself a redesigner.

I was fortunate enough to meet [designer brand builder] Mohan Murjani. And he said, "So what are you doing? I hear you're freelance design." He said, "Come with me and we'll start Tommy . . . what is your last name again?"

We started Tommy Hilfiger in 1985. There was Calvin doing putty black and gray, there was Perry Ellis doing some really cool stuff, and Ralph Lauren was doing his. But I thought that if I do mine the way I really wanted to do mine, I could compete with those guys.

Murjani said, "I want to introduce you to this advertising guy George Lois." He was this big guy with this loud mouth. Lois said, "So what's goin' on here?" A couple of days later he came back with these big ad layout boards. He had a picture of Ralph Lauren with a big X through it and a picture of Calvin Klein with a big X through it. He turned the board around and there was a picture of me, and he said, "This is the new!" I about had a heart attack because, I told him, I'm not one of the great American designers. He said, "That's the point. Everybody's going to say, 'Who the hell is this kid?' Do you want people to know your name or not?" And I said, "Well, yeah, eventually." He said, "It'll take you twenty years to get known by doing what you want to do. Don't worry. I've got another idea."

So he brought the other idea; it was a billboard with a list of the initials of the three famous men's designers: RL, CK, PE—and my initials, TH. Well, we put the billboard up in Times Square, and I was so embarrassed. There's no way I could hold a candle to these other designers. Meanwhile, I'm boasting that I'm one of them.

The phones started ringing off the hook—the *New York Times*, the *Wall Street Journal*, *Time*, *Newsweek*, *CNN*—everybody wanted to know who the hell this person was.

I saw my future. I pictured it. I didn't quite know how to get there, but I knew that I should never give up.

I came from a family with nine children in a very small town with very hard-working parents who struggled to pay the bills. I never wanted to be in that position.

1952

NILE
RODGERS

ISABELLA
ROSSELLINI

CHRISTOPHER
REEVE

S. EPATHA
MERKERSON

DAVID
BYRNE

AMY
TAN
AUTHOR

Amy Tan

My mother didn't teach me lessons about being Chinese as strongly as she did the notion of who I was as a female. I used to think that I didn't have dates because I was ugly, and I was ugly because I was Chinese. It's a terrible thing to think. It didn't help that my mother thought she was being honest and helpful by telling me that I was not beautiful. But it was good because I grew up also thinking that I could never rely on my looks as a way to get ahead in the world.

New York City, March 2014

My father and my brother died less than six months apart of brain tumors. I remember my father, from the childhood perspective, that he was perfect. And, that he, by dying, he abandoned me. When I was growing up, we moved about once a year. My mother's idea of the American dream was to move up in the world, to move into a better house, to have these symbols. I was a lonely child because I had lost my friends and so I wrote letters to the friends I left behind. I think it made for a miserable childhood, but it made for a good training ground for a writer.

Being a Chinese American often made me feel shameful. I had a perception of China that was very much the stereotype of the Fifties and Sixties, that people were largely peasants or communists. I had to go through a period of rebellion. In college I became an activist, insistent that we are just as valuable as anyone else.

My mother raised me to think that I was not equal to a man—but that I was better. That is something that women had to strive for as women's liberation was happening.

The drug back then was mushrooms. My mother hired a detective to have my boyfriend arrested. I got arrested along with all the other people who were my friends at the time. That's how fierce my mother was.

I then became an American Baptist scholar known for my good morals, my hard work. It's the experience of an immigrant. You leave a certain history behind you and you get to start over.

You would think that a Chinese mother would be more conservative. She could be very critical, but I think of my mother as very modern. My mother raised me to think that I was not equal to a man—but that I was better. That is something that women had to strive for as women's liberation was happening. I didn't have to battle within myself that that was the right notion.

I was thirty-seven when my first book was published. So I was very late in coming to publishing. But it also took me a long time to realize that that was the meaning of my life. I have questions always in my mind. And I think that they would have driven me crazy if I didn't have a way to explore them myself. Writing fiction, writing a story, is a way of meditating on the question and finding one possible answer.

I've always thought about death every day of my life. It's not with fear. It's with the knowledge that I only have a certain amount of time. When I turned sixty, I made that decision to go to the place that had the greatest marine biodiversity, and I knew I was going to see a shark. Swimming to a shark, you discover not just the beauty of a shark, you discover something in yourself that you have closed off.

You have a little less time now. But make it quality time. Make it richer time.

1953

JOHN MALKOVICH

ERIC BOGOSIAN

KATHIE LEE GIFFORD

KEN BURNS

RON JEREMY

EVE
ENSLER
PLAYWRIGHT

Eve Ensler

If my label were to say anything, it would be "Made in the Sixties." It was the time of hippies, sex, drugs, and rock and roll—completely defined, created, and determined by the lack of boundaries, the breaking through walls. It was an incredible time to come to consciousness because the country was coming to consciousness.

New York City, March 2014

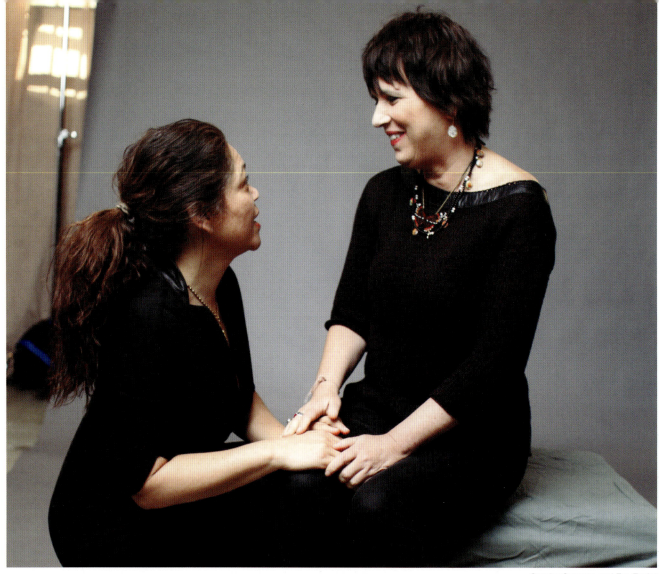

Sandra Guzman and Eve Ensler

Bob Dylan and Leonard Cohen and rock and roll, that was gospel to me. Motown—I think about Marvin Gaye and "Sexual Healing." What a radical idea that sex was healing. I learned my politics through that music.

I didn't see myself as a young feminist. So much of my childhood, to be honest, was about surviving violence. In that sense, sex, drugs, and rock and roll couldn't have come at a better time because all of those things were a way out of this body, out of feeling, out of the lie that was really being told, which was that I was growing up in this wonderful environment, with the corporate father and the blond mother. Everything appeared perfect on the outside when it was absolutely mad and violent and horribly abusive on the inside.

I would drive down to Manhattan and go to the Fillmore East. I had all these female icons, like Grace Slick, like Tina Turner, women who were breaking out of everything, who were breaking out of all the norms, who were fantastically talented. I had this dream that I would do in writing what they did in rock and roll.

I feel like feminism is a given. Do you want equal rights? Do you want equal pay? Every woman I talk to says yes, so it's not even an argument. Of course you're a feminist. But I think sometimes language just gets us so caught. How do we look at a new feminism? How are we evolving in terms of women's liberation and the liberation of the spirit and the liberation of consciousness that contains all this?

The Vagina Monologues began as curiosity. When I started performing, I had no idea what I was doing. But then I started to begin to understand what I was doing as I was performing it. I remember vividly one night at the Westside Arts Theater I actually had the experience of landing in my vagina. It was just like, "Whew." When I had that experience that first night of landing in myself, it was like I was whole.

I was making $18,000 a year before *The Vagina Monologues* happened, so to have any money was crazy. We made a decision that $5 of every ticket would go to ending violence against women and girls. Women and communities ranging from Islamabad to Alabama—equally scary—have done the play, and have been able to raise, through their efforts, $100 million over the last sixteen years.

There are some languages where they barely have words for vagina. I don't think there is an anatomical word, for example, in Hebrew for vagina. I don't believe there is a real word in Chinese either, only slang. Language is so powerful in that sense. You know, if we don't say something, if we don't utter it, then it doesn't exist.

I feel like feminism is a given. Do you want equal rights? Do you want equal pay? Every woman I talk to says yes, so it's not even an argument. Of course you're a feminist.

Theater has this incredible power like no other art form to embody thought, to embody ideas.

The Sixties were a particularly fervent time. People had a vision. They had a moral understanding and a moral direction. I miss music and I miss art that informed our souls but also gave us hope and gave us a political vision that we could struggle for.

1954

CHRISTIE
BRINKLEY

CINDY
SHERMAN

REV. AL
SHARPTON

TRUDIE
STYLER

CARLY
FIORINA

JULIEANNA RICHARDSON
FOUNDER, THE HISTORYMAKERS

Julieanna Richardson

The turbulence of the 1960s set the ground for our generation to really soar. There's no doubt that we are the beneficiaries of those who came before us. We are the affirmative action babies.

New York City, June 2014

We thought that we could rule the world in many ways. And I don't think we saw a glass ceiling. Back then, the only things that we studied about black people were George Washington Carver and slavery.

Our teacher comes into the classroom and she has an assignment that we tell about our family background. Everybody raises their hand. One student says, "I'm German." "I'm English," says another. It gets to me and I say I am Indian and French. The teacher looks at me like, "You fraud." Or that's how I felt. And that feeling really stayed with me. I needed to know that we had a history that was profound.

I was raised by an adoring father. I was a daddy's girl. My father was bragging in this little coal mining town that his daughter was going to go to Harvard Law School.

I was getting ready to go to college. My father asked me, "What are you gonna do?" I answered, "Are you crazy? Theater!" I told him that theater was the only thing I wanted to do in my life. And he said, "No, you have to do something more." My father told me, "You can do anything with a law degree."

It was 1980. Chicago was brimming with its blackness, and I wanted to be in the center of that. My coming out of Harvard Law School was a big deal. Who is this girl? She went to Harvard Law School? That was really my calling card. They just really took me in. There was great pride, great, great pride. We were entering the corporate arena in places that they could only have hoped to be.

The HistoryMakers is the largest video oral history archive in the country. When I started the project, some friends of mine had an intervention. They challenged me to answer two questions: Does an archive like the one you're envisioning exist already? And if it doesn't but one was to be created, would anyone be interested? "We," they said, "theorize no."

Our collection gives 9,000 hours of testimony. We are going into the Library of Congress. It will be our permanent

Julieanna Richardson and Chad Thompson

repository. Only once in the history of the United States had there been a massive attempt to record the black experience in the first voice. That was with the WPA Slave Narratives.

I was born 1954, the year of Brown v. Board of Education. There was tremendous hope of what integration would give our community. And I'm a beneficiary of that dream.

Last year I visited a school in Washington, D.C. It was totally segregated. It was totally black. And it was totally unequal. I worry about us and what my generation's legacy will be.

I realized my father's dream. I was the hope and the promise for what my father wanted. And so I have a responsibility. That's what I'm passionate about, to live out the rest of my years, to contribute, and to realize this American dream.

> We thought that we could rule the world in many ways. And I don't think we saw a glass ceiling.

1955

BILL
GATES

WHOOPI
GOLDBERG

JEFF
KOONS

SANDRA
BERNHARD

PENN
JILLETTE

MARIA SHRIVER
JOURNALIST

Maria Shriver

I come from a large, Irish Catholic, competitive family where everybody wants to make an impact in the world, even though there have been times when I would have thought, "Lord, this is a crazy group of people." But I feel really blessed to have grown up in a family where people expected you to go out and change the world, encouraged you to do so, and actually demanded it of you.

Los Angeles, May 2014

The Sixties were a turbulent time in American history and certainly in my own family. Both of my parents believed that they could change the world. And they believed that everybody who walked in our front door could also do that whether you were ten or twelve or eighty. Kids used to say, "I don't really want to come over to your house because your mother is going to make me volunteer and we're going to have to live on an Indian reservation or go to Africa. I really don't want to come over."

My dad ran the Peace Corps. He ran the War on Poverty, started legal services for the poor, Head Start. My mom was with Special Olympics and the Kennedy Foundation. They didn't have a bracelet that said, "What would Jesus do?" But I think it was kind of in their psyche. They went to mass every single day until they died.

I've always been an incredibly curious person. My dad was running for vice president and I had the opportunity to travel with him on the campaign trail. I ended up in the back of the plane where all the journalists were. And I realized that the people in the back of the plane were having a lot more impact on the campaign than my dad and his team. There was only one woman journalist, and that was both exciting and scary. But I wanted to be a journalist.

When I went into the newsroom at KYW in Philadelphia I was a person that logged other people's tapes. I went out with reporters. I spent several years working as a producer before I finally got the

> Both of my parents believed that they could change the world. And they believed that everybody who walked in our front door could also do that whether you were ten or twelve or eighty.

courage to go on camera. I went to the *CBS Morning News* and worked my way up to being an anchor. I got fired; the whole show got fired. Then I moved to NBC, where I spent 25 years.

I was raised by a formidable woman. She always pushed me to be competitive in a man's world. That was maybe one of the attractions to journalism in the beginning. It was a male profession, and I was comfortable in that.

I was scared to be a mom because I didn't think I was going to do it right. I wondered: Am I going to be able to cuddle and spend time and be happy going to Mommy and Me?

Each time I had a child, my professional life kind of dropped down a little. At one point I went to the president of NBC News and said, "I'm anchoring the Saturday *Nightly News,* and I'm anchoring *Sunday Today*, and one's in New York and one's in Washington and I live in Los Angeles." I asked if they would move one of the anchor jobs to the L.A. bureau because, I said, "I'm going to have to quit if you can't." And he said, "Well, go ahead, quit." So I did. And my jobs were filled in about, I think, maybe three seconds.

As First Lady of California I ran what became the largest women's conference in the world. And I thought, "What if I do a report and actually find out who the American woman is? How many women are working? What do they need, and what do they expect from government, from faith-based institutions, from men?" There hadn't been a national report since Eleanor Roosevelt did one for my uncle when he was president in 1963.

One of my Shriver Reports lays out that one in three American working women are on the brink of economic insecurity. That's a very different image than when my dad launched the War on Poverty with Lyndon Johnson.

I used to think that when I got a job people would stop asking me, "What's next?" And then when I wrote a book and I'd be at a book signing, people would come up to me and ask, "So, what's next?" It happens after you give birth to a child: People see the baby and comment, "When's the next one?"

My generation is known for being in a hurry to be the first to do everything, and it has made us a nation in a rush. We should take a beat and think about how best to use our talents right now, today.

1956

KAREN FINLEY | TOM HANKS | JERRY HALL | JEFFREY IMMELT | ANN MAGNUSON

KIM
CATTRALL
ACTOR

Kim Cattrall

My true love is my work. It's the thing that makes me the happiest. It's always taken me by the hand and led me to extraordinary experiences and circumstances—telling stories about being human and how vulnerable and frail we all really are, as well as how strong we can be.

New York City, June 2014

I went to theater school at the American Academy. I told myself, "If in seven years I haven't moved further than I am now, I'll go to typing school and become a secretary." Because that was still a job you could get back then.

Right out of the gate I got a contract with Otto Preminger. And I was in the south of France with Peter O'Toole and Isabelle Huppert making this really terrible film called *Rosebud*. When it came out it was called *Rose-dud* by *Time* magazine. People kept coming up and saying to me, "Does this have anything to do with *Citizen Kane*?" I had no idea who Orson Welles was at the time.

I made a deal with myself to be an artist, but also to be a businesswoman. I took *Porky's* to pay my rent because I didn't have any money. Now, when people say, "Oh my God, *Porky's* is so iconic," I think, "Yeah, it paid my rent for six months."

As a young actress and as a young woman, it was very frustrating because if we stood up for what we believed, we were thought of as being difficult or a bitch. And then the word passionate got introduced, as in "She's just passionate," meaning emotional or unpredictable. I developed a kind of real understanding when that was going on, and navigating that.

Early on in my career I signed with a very small agency. They asked me, "Do you dance?" I said, "Yes, I do a little tap." And they said, "Would you pole dance?" I thought, "Oh, I am in the wrong office." But I also thought to myself that if there had been different circumstances, that could have been my life, my trajectory.

> What changed for all of us was the AIDS epidemic, and then sex became a very negative part of our lives.

In the Seventies and early Eighties in a very healthy way, sex was integrated into our lives. What changed for all of us was the AIDS epidemic, and then sex became a very negative part of our lives. You could die from having sex. So everybody sort of battened down the hatches and didn't talk about sex. Right-wing sensibility came to the fore. *Sex and the City* was instrumental in breaking that free, especially with the character of Samantha, who was a child of the Seventies. It really caught on as far as people's imagination of, "Yes, oh we forgot about that thing. Oh right, okay."

When you are offered a series, you don't know where it's going to go. I had been the sex bomb when I was younger, and that was to pay the rent. And I thought, "I'm in my forties now, I want to be this way." But then I thought, "I am imposing an ageism on myself. Why can't I open up my mind and play this character in a way that could be joyful?"

My business, it's a visual medium. Where do you go in this society as a woman to age? I remember seeing Helen Mirren in the British series *Prime Suspect*. She had crow's feet, she had bags under her eyes, she was getting jowly. I thought to myself, "Wow, that's refreshing."

Women in their fifties and early sixties, we have so much to say. I have wrinkles. Let it be part of the story—as I sit here well lit!

1957

SPIKE
LEE

GLORIA
ESTEFAN

STEVE
BUSCEMI

KATIE
COURIC

DENIS
LEARY

VIRGINIA ROMETTY
CHAIRMAN, PRESIDENT & CEO, IBM

Virginia Rometty

Many people of our generation learned that it wasn't always what our parents said, it was what our parents did. I was in my teenage years when my parents were divorced and my mother was left alone with four children and faced with the prospects of no money, no home, no job. She went back to school. She worked at night. We all pitched in. We never saw my mother cry. We never saw her upset. My mother refused to let anyone define her as a failure. She wasn't going to be defined as a single mother. She was going to be defined—and have us be defined—by success. Between my brothers and sisters there are four of us, and we share six different degrees.

Armonk, NY, July 2014

> I never think of myself as being a woman CEO of this company. I think of myself as a steward of a great institution.

Some of the greatest influences were my teachers, and I actually think that says a lot about the generation and what was important. Like many, I remember the reaction of my teachers to the assassination of JFK and the importance of what they thought that meant to this country. It was one more thing that pointed to the influence that educators have on all of us.

I wasn't sure exactly what I wanted to do, but I always wanted to be the best at what I did. I always loved math and the sciences, which was a bit unusual for that time. Many people changed many majors. I never did. I stayed with engineering and with computer science. Those were the days when you would walk around with boxes of computer cards under your arm. It seems like a lifetime ago. And I would say that with the engineering, when I reflect back, it really helped people to problem solve, no matter what their passion was and what they went into. That's why I talk so much to young girls, to women, to anyone about going into engineering.

One of the most important things for any leader is to never let anyone else define who you are. You define who you are. I never think of myself as being a woman CEO of this company. I think of myself as a steward of a great institution.

As we grew up, we saw many things happen before our eyes. We learned that growth and comfort never coexist. That's true in the world around us, the price we pay for progress. It's true in our own careers. There are few times in a career when you can make an impact that will fundamentally change the way the world works.

The things we're working on are things like Watson, the world's first computer system that learns. One of the first things we set out to do was to help in the area of oncology and cancer. In our country alone, 85 percent of people with cancer will be treated at a regional type of hospital. I've watched Watson interact with the world's best doctors. You'd think they were interacting with a colleague. There's so much information, you can't remember all of it, no matter how smart you are. So just think of having a colleague who never forgets anything and then having been trained by some of the best doctors in the world by their case studies. That means the promise is there that within our lifetime everyone could have the gold standard of treatment for things like cancer.

Some of the characteristics of our generation are optimism and passion about what you do. We all grew up with this belief that we could do anything, that we could have an impact, and that it was always up to us.

1958

ALEC BALDWIN   **THURSTON MOORE**   **KEITH HARING**   **JAMIE LEE CURTIS**   **KEENEN IVORY WAYANS**

ELLEN
OCHOA

DIRECTOR, JOHNSON SPACE CENTER

Ellen Ochoa

I was born in 1958, the same year NASA was established, which I like to think of as not a coincidence. I was eleven years old when Apollo 11 landed on the moon. And, of course, everybody in the whole world was watching that, but at that time nobody ever asked a girl, "Is that something you want to grow up and do?" Women weren't part of the astronaut corps then. There were actually very few women involved at all in technical fields at NASA.

Houston, March 2014

At the high school my father went to, anybody who was Mexican was not allowed to use the swimming pool except on the day before the cleaners were going to come. As a result, my dad went off to the Naval Academy not knowing how to swim.

When my brothers, sisters, and I were growing up, my father didn't want to speak Spanish around the house. His feeling was that he just wanted his kids to fit in. I've wished over the years that I was bilingual because that's really a gift to be able to communicate with a much broader range of people.

A big moment in my life came in the eighth grade when, for the first time, girls were allowed to wear pants to our school. But there were all these rules. The pants had to be the same material as either a vest or a jacket. Of course, nobody had anything like that, so everybody went out and bought at least one pantsuit.

I don't think I was the rebellious kind. I was good in school. In the electrical engineering department at Stanford, there weren't a lot of women students. I went and talked to an electrical engineering professor, and I can say he was not at all encouraging. He would pick up these electrical components that were on his desk and say, "You'll have to work with these." Like he wasn't really sure that I would find that very interesting.

You get very used to feeling like you're standing out. I got the top grade in every physics class that I was in, and some of the professors seemed very surprised by that. Why shouldn't it be me? They didn't have to act quite so surprised. That is one thing about being in a science and engineering field: Your work speaks for itself.

Things changed so much from the time I was born to the time when I really began my career. I came around at just about the right time to be able to participate fully in space flight.

We had a press conference about ten days ahead of my first flight. One of the reporters asked me, "What are you most afraid about going into space?" And I said, "I'm most afraid of being in a car accident sometime in the next ten days and I don't get to go."

I've had the chance to fly on four different missions and almost a thousand hours in space. Things changed so much from the time I was born to the time when I really began my career. I came around at just about the right time to be able to participate fully in space flight.

One of the things that changed during my life was I didn't feel that I was limited, that I had to make choices. I could be an engineer. I could be an astronaut. I could be an inventor. I could be a mother. You're not shut out, and you're not just cast in one particular mold.

1959

KELLY
LYNCH

IRA
GLASS

PATRICIA
CLARKSON

EMERIL
LAGASSE

SUZANNE
VEGA

RONNIE
LOTT
ATHLETE

Ronnie Lott

The magic of sport is that you find yourself belonging. And you find yourself nurturing, and you find yourself wanting to serve and help to a point where you say, "I can. I can do that. I can be that."

San Francisco, June 2014

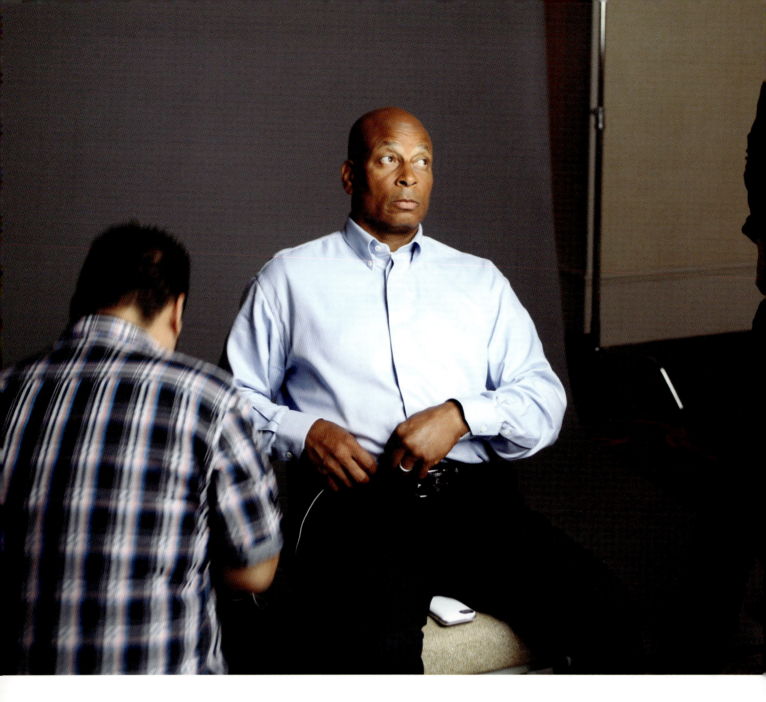

    You think of what people go through in any society to belong. I went to a march and saw Martin Luther King Jr. trying to rally people, to give them civil rights, to get people to fight.
    When I was a little kid, I went to go try out for a basketball team and the coach walked up to me and he said, "Can you play with white kids?" Really? I'll play with anybody. You've got to always be willing to go and say, "Hey man, let's see if we can do this." That's what Branch Rickey did with Jackie Robinson. That's how Pee Wee Reese broke it.
    Those moments are humbling because the best teammates are the guys who will give you their shirt off their back. Joe Montana was a great teammate, not because he could throw the football but because he could share his soul.
    You have to exhaust life and you have to know that you gave everything. Intensity—not only did it separate me when I played the game, but it also provided me all that goes into being consumed by being the best. It's a great feeling. It's wonderful. It's dangerous.

I went for a routine tackle against Timmy Newsome. His helmet hit my finger and when it hit the finger, the tip of the finger was lost. The next week was a playoff game against the Giants. The doctors said, "There's no way that you could play with your finger like that." The story goes that I took a machete and I tried to cut it off. No, I didn't take a machete. I ended up playing the following week. And I ended up having the fingertip amputated after the season.

We all have had those moments of surrendering to something.

Once you win one Super Bowl, you want more. Once you win two, you want more. Even once you've won four, you want more. Not winning the fifth was probably one of the most painful moments in my life. And not to ever revisit that again, that's a tough one.

Trying to be the best. Failing. Getting back up. Those characteristics are going to allow you to make great decisions. They are going to allow you to compete. They are going to allow you to achieve your best. That's the American dream. The American dream is not having a house. The American dream is exhibiting those kinds of qualities each and every day even if you don't have anything.

> When I was a little kid, I went to go try out for a basketball team and the coach walked up to me and he said, "Can you play with white kids?" Really? I'll play with anybody.

1960

ROBIN ROBERTS · MARIO BATALI · JULIANNE MOORE · TIMOTHY HUTTON · CAROL ALT

ERIN
BROCKOVICH
ENVIRONMENTALIST

Erin Brockovich

Have you ever smelled fresh-cut grass? It's fabulous. I learned everything being born and raised in Kansas. It was simple. It was value-driven. Respect. Honor. Integrity. Life for me growing up was easy, it was fun, it was outdoors, but it was also complicated. I am dyslexic. School wasn't my favorite thing. So I always had to figure out ways, you know? If a door closed, you'd open a window.

Los Angeles, March 2014

It can be somebody else's opinion to see you as a loser, but what matters is that you don't have to have that opinion.

There is a social justice component to the law. And that's one thing that really perplexed me about the legal case that was portrayed in the movie about me. The town of Hinkley was suing PG&E, which was trying to buy the property from this family. There's a real estate transaction going on. So why are there medical records in a real estate transaction? I'm going to sell my own house here soon. Am I going to put my medical records in there? I don't think so.

"You're not a scientist." "You're not a doctor." "You're not a lawyer." So therefore, what? I should shut up? They weren't told the truth. Everything that was important to them was being taken from them—clean water, their land, their homes, their health, their children. I know what's right, and I know what's wrong. Period. And that gave me confidence.

Had there not been the film, my name would not represent somebody who's out there fighting for the environment. People asked, "What are they going to call the movie?" And I said, "Well, it's *Erin Brockovich*." And some replied, "That's a stupid name for a movie." So I went and asked [director] Steven Soderbergh, "What's the name of the movie?" And he said, "*Erin Brockovich*." I was like, shit. Come on, I'm from Kansas. I'm not part of this Hollywood experience.

I remember as we were walking to the red carpet at the premiere, I turned the corner and Steven gave

me this little push. It was like, "You better get over it." Boom. And I stepped out there and it was like *whooosh*. I couldn't even see.

I wish I could tell you that it was like a dream come true. But that isn't my fairy tale. That isn't what I was dreaming. *Erin Brockovich* isn't about me. *Erin Brockovich* is about us all.

From Hinkley to today, our environmental policies, they're absent, they're overwhelmed, they're broken. There are so many rules on the books. Here's what I say: Enforce what you have on the books.

My fighting spirit definitely came from my being dyslexic. Behind me were a steadfast mom and dad who taught me about stick-to-it-iveness. *Definition: noun; dogged persistence born of obligation and stubbornness.* Destroying the environment, deceiving people, jeopardizing their health and their welfare is absolutely wrong. And if you wanna corner them, you're gonna corner me, and I come out swinging.

I am dyslexic. School wasn't my favorite thing. So I always had to figure out ways, you know? If a door closed, you'd open a window.

1961

LAURENCE FISHBURNE

ISAAC MIZRAHI

MARIA HINOJOSA

WAYNE GRETZKY

GEORGE LOPEZ

PETER
STALEY
AIDS ACTIVIST

Peter Staley

I came at the tail end of a generation that saw a lot of challenges and great change in this country. AIDS forced the gay community out of the closet. It's one of the great American civil disobedience movements.

New York City, July 2014

I knew full well from how I had grown up that I was entering a world that would not allow me to be open about who I was.

While I think I was infected in 1983, I didn't find out until they had discovered the HIV virus in 1985. I was already immune-suppressed and probably only had a couple years in front of me. I went home that Thanksgiving, just a week or two after I got the news, and had the hardest conversation of my life.

I got lucky. My family rallied. I didn't face rejection like a lot of my friends whose families had withdrawn their love.

But it took a while for the gay community to work up a level of indignation and anger to daringly come out and go in front of the cameras and scream for some action.

As I was walking to work, I got handed a flyer about an AIDS demonstration. When I went home that night and turned on the news, there was the demonstration by this new group, ACT UP, the AIDS

I got lucky. My family rallied. I didn't face rejection like a lot of my friends whose families had withdrawn their love.

Tommy Walker and Peter Staley

Coalition to Unleash Power. And there was Reagan's FDA commissioner responding with some policy tweak. And I was like, "Wow, I want a piece of that."

I became more and more public in ACT UP, appearing on news segments and being outrageous at the demonstrations; that's how most of my high school friends found out I was gay. It's a good way to tell people, actually, because you're doing something you love and it's a very powerful action.

My family watched me come out to all of their friends in this same way. I'm sure there were moments of pause and qualms and uncomfortableness, but my family never showed it.

We guilt-tripped the entire country about letting us die. Within three years of ACT UP being founded, the NIH research budget had tripled. That's how quickly we shifted things.

When very few in the straight world were willing to do so, Mathilde Krim, this amazing heterosexual socialite scientist, dedicated her entire life to AIDS. When you look at somebody like Elizabeth Taylor, the fact that she started doing it in 1985 is just extraordinary to me. The self-disclosure by Magic Johnson of his HIV status, it really brought home to America that it was hitting the African American community, it was hitting heterosexuals—it was a virus that didn't discriminate.

AIDS was our plague. By 1983, there were hundreds of cases. By 1985, there were thousands of cases. Thirty-six million have died. Thirty-five million are living with HIV somewhere in the world. And I'm one of them.

1962

KATE
SPADE

PATRICK
EWING

PAULA
ABDUL

MATTHEW
BRODERICK

JODIE
FOSTER

ROSIE
O'DONNELL
ENTERTAINER

Rosie O'Donnell

Television really started to take off when we were children. At first, not every family on the block had a television, never mind a color one. Then the neighbors got a remote control one, and all of a sudden TV became a very prominent force in our life and family. It also was unifying nationally. We all watched *M*A*S*H*, *All in the Family*, *Welcome Back, Kotter*.

New York City, August 2014

We all were brought into the consciousness of what was happening in our country by a fourth estate. There was a war in Vietnam, the first war that was televised. When Walter Cronkite said there was no way we could win the war, it meant something.

I'm the middle of five children. We were born Irish Catholic, one right after another. In 1973, when I was ten years old, my mother died of breast cancer. We weren't told that it was breast cancer. We were told that she had hepatitis. I went to the school library and looked it up. It said a disease people get from dirty needles, and I thought it was from sewing.

Catholicism was very important to both my father and my mother. We went to mass every Sunday. My father took us to mass shortly after my mother had died. There was part of the Catholic mass when the priest said, "And to those who have gone before us in the hope of rising again, especially Roseanne O'Donnell." And my brother started to cry. My father took us out of the church and we never went back.

There have been times in my adult life where I sought out the comfort of the Catholic church, including as recently as two years ago when I had a heart attack. But I always felt such comfort in the homes of the Jewish kids I grew up with. I loved going to Laurie Shachtner's house—the white shag rug, the serving dishes. Her mother always looked perfect. Oh, my God, she would grab me and hug me and say, "Oh, look at my shaina maidel, look at your punim." I heard "I love you" in the Jewish houses. It was so different from my house, where those words were never spoken.

My love of Barbra Streisand comes from my mother's love of Barbra Streisand. She came and stayed at my house once in 2006. I was not in my house. The entire time I was calling the woman who works for me. "Maria, dónde está Babra?" "Miss Rosie, she is by the pool in the backyard sitting on one of the lounge chairs." "You get that lounge chair and you put it in the garage! And you put crime scene tape around that! You don't let anyone sit on that till I get back!" The fact that she was in my house was almost too much for me to believe.

Long Island public school teachers saved my life. They were involved and invested and helpful. They took me to therapy; one even took me to a gynecologist.

One teacher took me into her family and loved me back to life. I remember being in the eighth grade, and she hugged

me, but I didn't know what to do with my hands. She said, "You know how to hug? You put your arms up, put 'em around, and squeeze." She taught me that love is not formed by blood, and families are not formed by blood, but rather it is love that makes a family.

When you are a child and experience something like the death of a parent, everything else feels like a speed bump. The mountain of grief that comes when your mother dies when you are ten years old is indescribable unless you've lived it.

When I knew I was gay, which for me was when I was sixteen or seventeen, I knew I was gay. I had my driver's permit, and I would drive around in my car with the windows rolled up. I'd be driving alone and saying out loud, "I am gay. I'm a gay person." I just wanted to get used to saying it. I never felt that I had to hide it, but I also never felt that I wanted to really share it.

To think how far we have come in just my lifetime; I never thought that we would get to where we are right now in terms of homosexual acceptance and rights.

I got married, in part, as an act to say: You should not force a pink triangle on people and think less of them—but if you are, then for God's sake give me mine and I will stand among them. Because you have no right to do this in a country with liberty and justice for all.

When my son Parker was a little boy, I was getting dressed to go out one night after working all day. He wanted to watch a video, and he was crying. I said, "Honey, I have to go. There are some children who don't have any medicine, and we're going to take care of those kids." And Parker turned to me and said, "Why don't you just stay home and take care of me?" In that moment I realized that it doesn't do anyone any good if you are not able to take care of yourself or your own. I've tried to find that balance in my life, and it hasn't always been easy.

> Love is not formed by blood, and families are not formed by blood, but rather it is love that makes a family.

1963

CONAN
O'BRIEN

VANESSA
WILLIAMS

HAKEEM
OLAJUWON

EDIE
FALCO

SUZAN-LORI
PARKS

DAVID LACHAPELLE
ARTIST

David LaChapelle

My mom was an immigrant from Lithuania. She came the last year Ellis Island was open. She had this idea of America and what it should be like. And although we were middle class, she would photograph us as a family in front of other people's homes, and country clubs we didn't belong to, and cars that weren't ours.

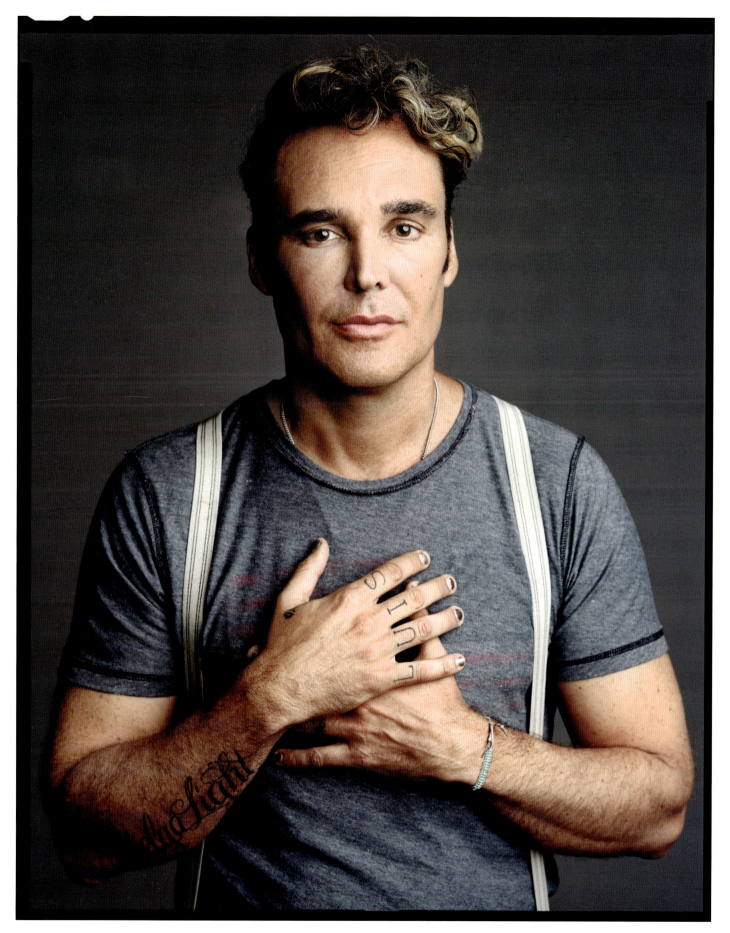

Los Angeles, June 2014

She was incredible, my mom. She showed me a picture of Ursula Andress once in *Playboy*. "This is what a woman's body should look like." There's much more to our physical beings than how hot we look.

I was going to be a painter until I picked up a camera. My first roll of film was of stairs, light hitting them, crack in the wall, and then by the sixteenth frame all my friends had their clothes off, and they were all in these Renaissance poses.

Going to public high school was horrendous; getting milk cartons thrown at me. I just dropped out of school. In Connecticut, yeah, it was a big, huge issue that I was different, and that I was a faggot, that I was gay. But when I came to New York, it wasn't an issue at all.

I knew that there was a place for me somewhere because I'd read about these artists. I had a picture of Elton John in my bedroom and I saw him in all these crazy feathers and hats, and I just thought, "Well, you know, he looks different." For all the reasons that they didn't like me in school, I was liked in New York City.

I met Andy Warhol at this club where the Psychedelic Furs were playing. I said I was a photographer. He said, "Well, come by and show me your photographs." I loved Andy. He was one of my heroes. I was super blown away. Bridget Polk was at the front desk, and she just rolled her eyes—another twink comin' to visit Andy, you know.

I remember him looking at the photographs of my naked high school friends, and he said, "These are great. These are great." He liked the energy of young people. He liked the energy of Jean-Michel Basquiat and Keith Haring, all of us. He gave us—so many people—their first jobs. It was very magical.

> She showed me a picture of Ursula Andress once in *Playboy*. "This is what a woman's body should look like." There's much more to our physical beings than how hot we look.

Things were very grungy at this time. AIDS had weighed everyone down, including myself. My first real boyfriend that I lived with, Louis Albert, died when he was twenty-four. I was twenty-one. He died so quickly. It was a matter of weeks. He went from dancing in this Melvin Van Peebles show about Bessie Smith called *Champeen*—my parents were there and Louis was incredible—and just a few weeks later he was dead.

For years, I blocked out the memories. If I look at that time and what kind of pictures I was doing, I wanted to see explosive color, and I wanted escapism, and fantasy, and a journey away from reality.

I don't take pictures with a cell phone. There's not really any candid shot. It turns into a big shoot. I can't stop, I'd just keep shooting, and shooting, and shooting. I'd be with my family saying, "Aunt Louise, take your top off and lay down on the floor!" Everything turns into a big shoot.

I never set out to shock anybody. What's shocking is cruelty and torture, and that's become our entertainment. Kids can play violent video games, but God forbid they look at a naked woman. That's pornography, that's perverse. No!

In whatever way I can, I'm trying to rescue the nude. To be an artist, it's a blessing, yet it's a responsibility. To me, the picture's not finished until that magical thing happens when someone looks at it and you're communicating. They have this moment with your work, and you're connecting without words. And that's really, really beautiful.

1964

MICHELLE
OBAMA

COURTENEY
COX

MATT
DILLON

ROSIE
PEREZ

WANDA
SYKES

JOHN
LEGUIZAMO
ACTOR

John Leguizamo

The Sixties helped break down that Fifties mentality, everybody trying to fit in, and that was the beginning of people exploring themselves, exploring feelings, and exploring a different way of living and sharing life. By the time it got to the Seventies, I guess that dream kind of crumbled a little bit, but it became much more exciting. I don't know about the Eighties. I'm not really sure.

New York City, May 2014

We all have nostalgia for the old, dirty, messed up New York. You didn't know how special it was, but you knew it was exciting. Disco happened, and then you started edging into hip-hop and break dancing, which was a whole new urban experience.

Queens was a little different because I guess it was the last white bastion. And you saw the poor Irish, Italians, and Jews leaving because we were coming and coming. It was still great. We still all mixed and got to hang out with their daughters and mess with them before they left.

My family is obviously light-skinned, but I still felt racism. When I had my afro when I was fourteen and we'd go to a fancy restaurant, they would put us all the way in the back, right next to the kitchen. And my father would say, "Because of your afro. If you would cut that off, we would be sitting in the front." To which I'd say, "Good luck with that."

I wasn't supposed to make it. I just wasn't. Not statistically. I didn't see my people anywhere that was important, except in the news, which is where you don't want to be. I just didn't feel like I was part of the American fabric. And my friends and I, we just felt like, "That ain't gonna happen for us. That ain't even for us. We just—what we have is here, us. Let's just have fun. Let's have a goof. We're just gonna enjoy our life right now because that's all we got."

> I wasn't supposed to make it. I just wasn't. Not statistically. I didn't see my people anywhere that was important, except in the news, which is where you don't want to be.

My generation started to understand that if you worked hard enough, anything was possible. You knew somewhere in the back of your mind that was it. My best friend, Crash, who was doing graffiti all over the city, he was Picasso to us. And Crazy Legs—he'd bring his cardboard, his linoleum, and he like invented break dancing. People were inventing stuff. We were creative. You know, just because you didn't have something didn't mean you couldn't make something up.

I didn't start acting because I wanted to be famous. I did it because it made me feel good. But every audition I would go to, it'd be me, Benicio Del Toro, Luis Guzmán, Benjamin Bratt, and it was either for a drug dealer, a murderer, or a janitor. What was that, that we could only play these minimal roles? If there was a really great Latin role, it didn't go to us. It went to, you know, Pacino or De Niro.

I just knew that Latin people were really funny. My family was really funny, and we had incredible stories to tell. Where was that on TV? Where was that in movies? Where was that in plays? I mean, we were fucking funny and interesting. Why wasn't that happening? So that was kind of like my impetus for everything.

I would go to these performance art spaces downtown and I could write whatever I want. I could be the lead in my own stories. And all these white kids would be watching and they'd be laughing and I was like, "Oh my God, I found myself." I wanted to document my life. I wanted to have it on paper. I needed to have it in a concrete form because so much of my childhood was spent being invisible.

The importance of family comes from being Latin. Family is everything. I was always more of a serial monogamist than a straight-up player. I wanted to have kids. I wanted to give them a life that was so different than my life, but I definitely wanted to give them a little adversity. You can't have happiness without pain.

What makes me happy is my therapist. Unfortunately, he sounds just like my dad, but on Xanax. He'll say, "You know, you have to be happy where you are. You don't have to be more or please anybody. Stop being so other-directed." Not being able to have what you want, that Zen of being happy with unhappiness. Pursuit of happiness—how about pursuit of just making it through the damn day. You know what I mean!

BIOGRAPHIES

TIM O'BRIEN (b. 1946) is a veteran of the Vietnam War and an award-winning author whose works include *The Things They Carried* and *Going After Cacciato*.

DEEPAK CHOPRA, M.D., (b. 1947) is a global leader and pioneer in the field of mind-body medicine and the author of more than 80 books.

SAMUEL L. JACKSON (b. 1948) is an Oscar-nominated actor and producer who has appeared in film classics ranging from *Jungle Fever* to *Pulp Fiction*.

BILLY JOEL (b. 1949) is a six-time Grammy Award-winning singer-songwriter who has sold more than 150 million records and had thirty-three Top 40 hits.

STEVE WOZNIAK (b. 1950) is an inventor, engineer, and philanthropist who co-founded Apple Computer.

TOMMY HILFIGER (b. 1951) is an American fashion designer whose eponymous apparel and accessories brand is known worldwide.

AMY TAN (b. 1952) is an award-winning writer whose best-known novel, *The Joy Luck Club*, was translated into thirty-five languages and adapted into a successful feature film.

EVE ENSLER (b. 1953) is a Tony Award-winning playwright, performer, author, and activist whose play *The Vagina Monologues* has been performed in more than 140 countries.

JULIEANNA RICHARDSON (b. 1954) is the founder and executive director of The HistoryMakers, the nation's largest collection of African American video oral histories.

MARIA SHRIVER (b. 1955) is a Peabody and Emmy Award-winning journalist and producer, as well as a *New York Times* best-selling author.

KIM CATTRALL (b. 1956) is an actor and producer whose career spans film, stage, and television, including the role of Samantha Jones on HBO's *Sex and the City*.

VIRGINIA ROMETTY (b. 1957) is chairman, president, and chief executive officer of IBM, where she began her career in 1981.

ELLEN OCHOA (b. 1958) is the director of the Johnson Space Center. She became the first Hispanic woman to go to space and is a veteran of four space flights.

RONNIE LOTT (b. 1959) is an NFL Hall of Famer and winner of four Super Bowls with the San Francisco 49ers.

ERIN BROCKOVICH (b. 1960) is an environmental activist who was portrayed by actress Julia Roberts in the award-winning feature film *Erin Brockovich*.

PETER STALEY (b. 1961) is an AIDS and gay rights activist and early leader of the advocacy group ACT UP.

ROSIE O'DONNELL (b. 1962) is an Emmy and Tony Award-winning entertainer whose longtime philanthropic efforts have raised awareness for children's causes and LGBT equality.

DAVID LACHAPELLE (b. 1963) is an artist whose work includes fine art and commercial photography, music video, and documentary film.

JOHN LEGUIZAMO (b. 1964) is the Emmy Award-winning entertainer and comedian known for his film, television, and theater performances.

ACKNOWLEDGEMENTS

Most projects take years, with seemingly endless conversations, delicate cajoling, and complicated timing.

Sometimes the stars align perfectly.

From the moment I outlined *The Boomer List* concept to AARP's powerhouse Myrna Blyth—nineteen subjects, one born in each of the boomer years, telling disparate stories of the generation—she loved it. "Timothy, it must air in 2014 for this to work because by the end of the year, the last of the baby boomers will have turned fifty!"

Massive Excel spreadsheets materialized. Names were pulled from online databases, categorized by birthdate. We discovered, to our shock, that some people still lie about their age.

With the clock ticking, it was documentary doyenne Susan Lacy to the rescue. At a catch-up dinner at Omen, of all places, I mentioned *Boomer* to Susan. "This belongs at PBS! These are all American Masters."

Figuring out the right balance for *The Boomer List* was like working on a Rubik's Cube, in the dark. Our mission was to balance genders, diversity, and professions. Not so easy. For example, if we agreed on a musician for a certain year, that would close the door on other musicians in any other year.

Many people worked overtime on the film, the book, and the exhibition. They all have my thanks and gratitude. A few deserve an extra shout-out!

It was a pleasure working with everyone at AARP. In addition to Myrna, I want to thank, in particular, Karin Ballman and Jodi Lipson.

I'd like to especially acknowledge *American Masters* series creator Susan Lacy. Susan gave me my first opportunity to produce and direct with *Lou Reed: Rock and Roll Heart*. Nine films later, I'm back at PBS and delighted to work with Michael Kantor, Julie Sacks, Junko Tsunashima, Lesley Norman, Natasha Padilla, and Stephen Segaller.

A museum exhibition is a tremendous milestone for any artist. I'm honored to show my large-scale master portraits at the prestigious Newseum in Washington, D.C. Special thanks go out to the Newseum's Cathy Trost and Sonya Gavankar, as well as to Adamson Editions master printers David Adamson and John Hughs.

Luxury Custom Publishing was again wonderful to work with and did an exceptional job on this book. Thanks to Peter Gotfredson, Scott Gummer, Lauren Clulow, Nate Beale, Victoria Scavo, and Carolyn Saylor.

Core producers Tommy Walker and Chad Thompson, along with editor Charlie Watt Smith, worked tirelessly. Betsy Berg, Ingrid Duran, Catherine Pino, and Michael Slap Sloane added vital input and counsel. Karin Greenfield-Sanders' attention to detail was invaluable. Thank you all.

Lastly, I thank all the boomers who gave us their time, energy, and unique perspective on this remarkable generation. I send much love to Erin Brockovich, Kim Cattrall, Deepak Chopra, Eve Ensler, Tommy Hilfiger, Samuel L. Jackson, Billy Joel, David LaChapelle, John Leguizamo, Ronnie Lott, Tim O'Brien, Ellen Ochoa, Rosie O'Donnell, Julieanna Richardson, Virginia Rometty, Maria Shriver, Peter Staley, Amy Tan, and Steve Wozniak.

The *Boomer* project has been a great collaboration between my team, AARP, PBS, and the Newseum. As one of our boomers, artist David LaChapelle, would say, "I'm super blown away."

Copyright © 2014 Timothy Greenfield-Sanders
Master portraits © Timothy Greenfield-Sanders
AARP is a registered trademark

Pages 2-3: All photos by Timothy Greenfield-Sanders
Page 9: Jo Ann Jenkins by Miller Mobley
Page 126: Samuel L. Jackson

No part of this publication may be reproduced, stored in a retrieval system or transmitted in any form or by any means, electronic, mechanical, photocopying, recording, scanning or otherwise, except as permitted under Sections 107 or 108 of the 1976 United States Copyright Act, without either the prior written permission of the Publisher, or authorization through payment of the appropriate per-copy fee to the Copyright Clearance Center, 222 Rosewood Drive, Danvers, MA 01923, (978) 750-8400, fax (978) 646-8600. Requests to the Publisher for permission should be addressed to publisher@luxurycustompublishing.com

Limit of liability/disclaimer of warranty: AARP, Luxury Custom Publishing, and Timothy Greenfield-Sanders make no representations or warranties with respect to the accuracy or completeness of the contents of this work and specifically disclaim all warranties, including without limitation warranties of fitness for a particular purpose. The fact that an organization or company is referred to in this work does not mean that AARP, Luxury Custom Publishing, or Timothy Greenfield-Sanders endorses it.

AARP publishes a variety of print and e-books; please visit www.aarp.org/bookstore.

Bulk discounts for *The Boomer List* are available by contacting sales@luxurycustompublishing.com

Designed by Luxury Custom Publishing LLC, (888) 527-5556
Library of Congress Cataloging-in-Publication Data available

ISBN: 978-0-9906671-0-0

Printed in Hong Kong
10 9 8 7 6 5 4 3 2 1

LCP | LUXURY CUSTOM PUBLISHING
3920 Conde Street
San Diego, CA 92110
www.luxurycustompublishing.com